Rain Forest Animals

ANIMALS IN THEIR HABITATS

June Randolph

PICTURE CREDITS
Cover: photographs of Parson's chameleon (top left), jaguar (middle left), leaf cutter ant (bottom left), red-eyed treefrog (bottom right), tarantula (top right).

cover: © Getty Images (top left and bottom left); page 1 © David A. Northcott/Corbis; page 8 (bottom left) © Getty Images; page 10 (bottom left) © ONF; page 10 (middle) © Joel Creed/Ecoscene/Corbis; page 11 © Wolfgang Kaehler/Corbis; page 12 © Tom Brakefield/Corbis; page 13 (top, middle) © Getty Images; page 13 (bottom) © Dennis Johnson/Papilo/Corbis; page 14 (bottom left) © Joe McDonald/Corbis; page 19 © Getty Images; page 20 (bottom left) © Jim Zuckerman/Corbis; page 21 (bottom left) © Mary Ann McDonald/Corbis; page 22 (left) © Kevin Schafer/Corbis; page 22 (right) © Getty Images; page 23 (bottom left) © Roger Wilmshurst/Frank Lane Picture Agency/Corbis; page 24 (top right) © George D. Lepp/Corbis; page 24 (bottom left) © Michael & Patricia Fogden/Corbis; page 25 (top right) © Martin Rogers/Corbis; page 25 (bottom left) © Getty Images; page 26 (bottom right) © Kevin Schafer/Corbis.

Produced through the worldwide resources of the National Geographic Society, John M. Fahey, Jr., President and Chief Executive Officer; Gilbert M. Grosvenor, Chairman of the Board; Nina D. Hoffman, Executive Vice President and President, Books and Education Publishing Group.

PREPARED BY NATIONAL GEOGRAPHIC SCHOOL PUBLISHING
Ericka Markman, Senior Vice President and President, Children's Books and Education Publishing Group; Steve Mico, Vice President and Editorial Director; Marianne Hiland, Executive Editor; Richard Easby, Editorial Manager; Jim Hiscott, Design Manager; Kristin Hanneman, Illustrations Manager; Matt Wascavage, Manager of Publishing Services; Sean Philpotts, Production Manager.

EDITORIAL MANAGEMENT
Morrison BookWorks, LLC

PROGRAM CONSULTANTS
Dr. Shirley V. Dickson, Program Director, Literacy, Education Commission of the States; James A. Shymansky, E. Desmond Lee Professor of Science Education, University of Missouri-St. Louis.

National Geographic Theme Sets program developed by Macmillan Education Australia, Pty Limited.

Published by the National Geographic Society
1145 17th Street, N.W.
Washington, D.C. 20036-4688

ISBN: 0-7922-4717-5

Product 41957

Printed in Hong Kong.

Contents

Animals
in Their Habitats

Think of all the animals in the world. Now think of all the places where animals live. The places where animals live are called habitats. Animals get all the things they need to live from their habitats. There are different kinds of habitats. Some are temperate forests, oceans, deserts, and rain forests.

 ## Key Concepts ....

1. **Animals interact with their environment and with other animals in their habitats.**

2. **There are many different habitats on Earth. Animals live in habitats that meet their needs.**

3. **Adaptations help animals survive in their habitats.**

Four Kinds of Habitat

Temperate Forest

Temperate forests are good habitats for animals like deer.

Ocean

Oceans are good habitats for animals like fish.

In this book you will learn about animals that live in rain forests like this one.

Desert

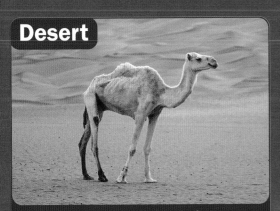

Deserts are good habitats for animals like camels.

Rain Forest

Rain forests are good habitats for animals like gorillas.

Animals of the Rain Forest

Enter a tropical rain forest and you may meet some of the most amazing animals on Earth. The largest snake in the world, the anaconda, lives in a rain forest. One of the world's slowest animals, the sloth, lives in a rain forest, too. So do poison arrow frogs and tarantula spiders. The rain forest habitat is a unique place.

Forecast: Rain

Tropical rain forests grow in hot places where it rains a lot. These forests are called tropical because they are mostly found between the Tropic of Cancer and the Tropic of Capricorn. In this region, the temperature stays warm. It is about 26° Celsius (80° Fahrenheit) year round. There is heavy rainfall. Rain forests get at least 198 centimeters (78 inches) of rain each year. Sometimes, however, the animals on the ground do not even know that it is raining. This is because the trees in a rain forest are so dense and tall, they act like a shield. They block the rain before it reaches the forest floor.

Poison arrow frogs

The warm, moist **climate** of a tropical rain forest is perfect for plant growth. In turn, the plants of the rain forest **habitat** feed and shelter many different kinds of creatures.

The largest area of tropical rain forest is in the Amazon region in South America. But Africa, Australia, India, Madagascar, and Southeast Asia have tropical rain forests, too.

Anacondas are the world's largest snakes.

habitat
the place where an animal or plant usually lives in nature

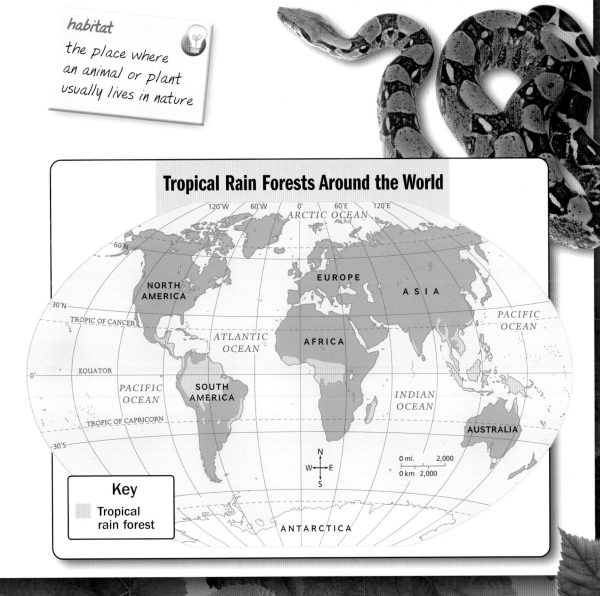

Tropical Rain Forests Around the World

Key
Tropical rain forest

Living in Levels

A rain forest has several levels. These levels provide food and shelter for the animals that live within the rain forest.

Millions of different animals live in a rain forest. Where they live in the rain forest depends on what they can do. For example, many large animals, such as tapirs, live at the forest floor level. The forest floor provides them with the food and shelter they need. But animals in the canopy must be able to fly or travel high in the branches. The spider monkey swings from tree to tree in search of the leaves and ripe fruits it eats. Most of the animals in the emergent level, such as birds and butterflies, are flyers, as they live high up in the trees.

Rain Forest Levels

Tapirs live on the forest floor, where they search for fallen fruits.

**60 meters
(200 feet)**

Emergent Level
At the emergent level, some trees are so tall that they emerge from, or rise above, the canopy. Birds are the largest inhabitants of the emergent level.

**35 meters
(115 feet)**

Canopy
High in the air, thick tree tops form a top, or canopy, that is like a huge living umbrella. The canopy is home to many different species. Sloths and howler monkeys live here.

**20 meters
(60 feet)**

Understory
Beneath the canopy are smaller trees and bushes. Only a little sunlight filters into this area. Small birds and reptiles live in the understory.

**1.8 meters
(6 feet)**

Forest Floor
The forest floor is a moist and shadowy place. Both tiny insects and large mammals live at the forest floor level.

Living Together

Millions of plants and animals live together in the rain forest habitat. So, how can so many different **organisms** live together in the same area? All the living things in the rain forest form a **community**. In that community, each member depends on others to survive. Each member also depends on the nonliving things in the rain forest. These include soil, water, and **oxygen**. All of these connections help keep the rain forest in balance. This way, it can support the many living things that depend on it.

community
a group of plants and animals living together in a habitat

Living Together in the Rain Forest

Jaguars and peccaries are part of the rain forest community. They need each other, and they need the plants around them.

Ripe figs provide food for the peccary when they fall to the forest floor.

The peccary is hunted on the forest floor by the jaguar.

What Every Animal Needs

Like all animals on Earth, rain forest animals need to have their basic needs fulfilled. They need food, shelter, water, and oxygen for survival. They find all of these things in their rain forest habitats.

In the rain forest, the mixture of rain and heat creates an ideal place for plants to grow. Trees flower and produce seeds all year round. The variety of plant life provides food for many kinds of animals. Some birds, bats, and insects eat only fruit and flower nectar. Other animals, such as sloths and monkeys, eat leaves. The plant-eating animals may, in turn, become food for meat-eating animals. These include jaguars and anacondas.

Finding water is not hard in the rain forest. In such a wet habitat, rivers, streams, and lush plants provide all the water the animals need.

The thick canopy and dense ground **foliage** of the rain forest shelter many creatures. They help them hide from enemies. Some species have special colors or patterns that help them hide in their plant shelters.

Millions of leaf cutter ants live on the forest floor. They use leaves to grow a special fungus for food.

Key Concept 3 Adaptations help animals survive in their habitats.

Adaptations

An **adaptation** is a special **trait** that helps an animal survive in its habitat. Some adaptations are **physical adaptations**. These involve parts of the body. Other adaptations are **behavioral adaptations**. They are the special things the animal does for food or protection.

> *adaptation*
> *a body part or the way an animal acts to help it survive*

Physical Adaptations There are many different types of physical adaptations that help animals find food and protect themselves. The anteater's long snout is an example of a physical adaptation. The long snout, along with its thin tongue, help the anteater find food to survive in the rain forest.

The jaguar is another example of an animal with a body suited to finding food in the rain forest. The jaguar is an excellent climber. This means it can hunt its prey from above. It is also a good swimmer. It can catch fish in the rivers found within rain forests.

The anteater uses its large, heavy claws to break open ants' nests. Then it uses its long snout and tongue to reach the ants inside.

Heavy, sharp claws

Long snout

Long, thin tongue

Many animals use physical adaptations to help keep safe from enemies. Many animals have body colors or shapes that let them blend into their surroundings. This is called **camouflage**. It helps animals hide from **predators**. An example of an animal that uses camouflage to keep safe is the green iguana. Its leaf-like green color and ability to keep very still make it hard to see in the rain forest.

The green iguana blends into the green rain forest habitat.

Some hunters use camouflage, too. The patterns on a jaguar's fur look like patches of sunlight and shadow in the rain forest. This means it can remain unnoticed by its prey as it gets ready to pounce.

A jaguar lies in wait for prey, hidden by its camouflage.

Some poisonous animals have bright colors that warn predators of their danger. Other animals just look like dangerous animals. This is called **mimicry**. For example, the hawk moth caterpillar looks like a dangerous snake.

The hawk moth caterpillar uses mimicry to ward off its enemies.

Behavioral Adaptations The kind of adaptation that has to do with the way an animal acts is called a behavioral adaptation. A behavioral adaptation is an **inherited** behavior. It is passed from one **generation** to the next. This means that an animal does not have to learn this behavior.

The great hornbill is a bird with an interesting inherited behavioral adaptation. Hornbills build their nests in tree holes. When the female is ready to lay her eggs, she seals herself into the nest with a layer of mud and other material. She leaves only a small slit as an opening. The male hornbill passes food to the female through the slit. The female stays inside her self-made prison until her

This male great hornbill is passing food to a female hornbill holed up in the nest.

babies are hatched. This behavior keeps her eggs safe from predators. Baby hornbills are born knowing how to seal up a nest. It is an adaptation that is passed from one generation to the next.

Other behaviors are learned. For example, a baby gorilla learns how to get food by watching older gorillas. Although this behavior will help the gorilla survive, it is not inherited. This means it is not an adaptation.

Baby gorillas learn by watching other gorillas.

Think About the **Key Concepts**

Think about what you read. Think about the pictures and diagrams. Use these to answer the questions. Share what you think with others.

1. How do animals and plants affect each other in the same habitat?

2. What things do all animals need?

3. How do animals get their needs met?

4. How do adaptations help animals meet their needs?

Cross-Section Diagram

Diagrams are pictures that show information.
You can learn new ideas without having to read a lot of words. Diagrams use pictures and words to explain ideas.

There are different kinds of diagrams.
This diagram of a leaf cutter ant nest is a **cross-section diagram**. A cross-section diagram is a picture that shows the inside of something. It helps show what something looks like if you cut it in half. Look back at the diagram on pages 8–9. It is a cross-section diagram of the levels of a rain forest.

How to Read a Diagram

1. **Read the title.**
   It tells you what the diagram is about.

2. **Read the labels and captions.**
   They tell you about the parts of the diagram.

3. **Study the picture.**
   The picture shows how the parts fit together.
   This diagram shows the inside of a leaf cutter ant nest.

4. **Think about what you learned.**
   Decide what new information you learned from the diagram.

Nest of the Leaf Cutter Ant

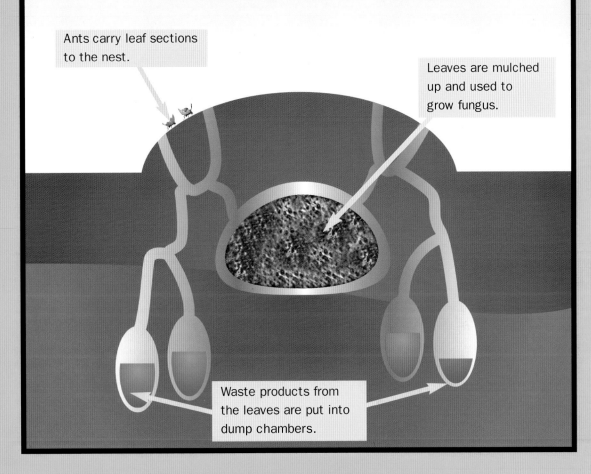

Leaf cutter ants "farm" their food. They cut leaves into small pieces, carry them to their nest, then use them to grow a special fungus.

Ants carry leaf sections to the nest.

Leaves are mulched up and used to grow fungus.

Waste products from the leaves are put into dump chambers.

What's Inside?

Read the diagram by following the steps on page 16. Write down all the things you found out about a leaf cutter ant nest. Share what you found out with a classmate. Compare what you learned. What is the same? What is different?

Reference Sources

The purpose of **reference sources** is to inform. Reference sources can take many forms.

You use different reference sources for different things. For example, if you want to know how to spell *echidna*, use a dictionary. But if you want to know what an echidna eats, use an **encyclopedia**.

You don't read a reference source from beginning to end. You read only the parts that cover topics you want to learn about.

Encyclopedia
of Rain Forest Animals

This sample shows an encyclopedia entry.
Encylopedias give basic facts about many topics.
All the entries in this encyclopedia are about
rain forest animals.

Anaconda

Title for each entry

- reptile
- found in South America
- lives in the understory

List of basic facts about the topic

The world's largest snake, the anaconda,
can grow to about 9 meters (30 feet)
long. When it is hungry, this powerful
snake wraps its body around its prey
and crushes the animal to death.
Then it eats the animal whole.

Text has important information.

Anacondas like to eat fish, birds, and
turtles. But sometimes very large
anacondas will eat animals that weigh
as much as 55 kilograms (121 pounds).
This snake has a physical adaptation
that allows it to eat something so big.
Its jaw can "unhinge" and open
very wide.

Photographs help
you picture what you
are reading.

Captions give
more information.

▲ An anaconda will often lie on a
branch above water, waiting to
drop down on its prey.

Echidna

- monotreme
  (a mammal that lays eggs)
- found in Australia and
  New Guinea
- lives on the forest floor

The echidna is one of only two monotremes in the world. It is also known as the spiny anteater. This is because it is covered with strong spines. If threatened by an enemy, the echidna can curl into a spiny ball. The echidna can also burrow into the ground if under threat.

The echidna eats insects found on the rain forest floor. It picks these up by extending its long, sticky tongue.

▲ The echidna's long, thin snout helps it root out food along the forest floor.

Golden Lion Tamarin

- mammal
- found in Brazil
- lives in the understory
  and canopy

This brightly colored animal is named for the mane that covers its head and shoulders like the mane of a lion. Using its wiry arms and long, nimble tail, the tamarin swings easily from tree to tree in search of insects, lizards, and birds. Its long, thin fingers and claws let it easily pull grubs from tree bark and crevices.

The golden lion tamarin is active by day. At night, it sleeps in old hollow trees.

◄ The golden lion tamarin has long golden hair on its body.

Gorilla

- mammal
- found in Africa
- lives in the understory and on the forest floor

The gorilla is the largest living ape in the world. A gorilla, like all apes, has arms that are longer and stronger than its legs. Gorillas use their powerful arms and legs to move quickly along the forest floor.

Gorillas spend most of their time browsing the forest floor, feeding on leaves and stalks of plants. They build nests to sleep in by bending the twigs and branches of trees.

▲ Gorillas use facial expressions, body gestures, and sounds to communicate.

Green Iguana

- reptile
- found in Central and South America
- lives mostly in the understory

This iguana lives in trees, but it is also a good swimmer. It uses its razor-sharp teeth and long claws to defend itself when attacked. It can also use its tail as a whip.

The female green iguana lays eggs in a hole in the ground. Here, the eggs take three months to hatch.

The young iguanas eat a greater variety of food than the adults. They feed on insects, fruits, flowers, and leaves.

▲ Most green iguanas have green skin, which provides camouflage in the understory.

◄ The howler monkey howls to inform other monkeys of its presence, or to send alarm signals.

▲ Hummingbirds have a muscular, compact body and small feet.

Howler Monkey

- mammal
- found in Central and South America
- lives in the canopy

Howler monkeys live high in the treetops of the rain forest. They mostly eat leaves. But sometimes they also eat fruit and maggots. The howler monkey's long, strong tail enables it to hang on to branches while using its hands and feet to get food.

The howler monkey is one of the noisiest animals in the world. When it calls out, a hollow bone in its throat makes the sound louder. It is said that a howler monkey's howl can be heard up to 4.8 kilometers (3 miles) away.

Hummingbird

- bird
- found in North and South America
- lives in the understory

The hummingbird is the smallest bird in the world. It gets its name from the noise its wings make as they beat up to 70 times a second.

There are many species of hummingbirds. The smallest is only about 5 centimeters (2 inches) long. The biggest is about 21 centimeters (8 inches) long. Some hummingbirds are among the most vividly colored birds in the world.

Jaguar

- mammal
- found in Central and South America
- lives mostly on the forest floor

The jaguar is one of the most powerful cats in the world. It is large and strong and can weigh up to 136 kilograms (300 pounds).

The jaguar is a very fast runner and an excellent hunter. It hunts mainly at night and eats almost any kind of animal it can find on the forest floor.

The jaguar has striking markings on its body. Many black or brown circles and spots stand out against its golden-orange fur.

▲ The name *jaguar* means "killer that takes its prey in a single leap."

Madagascan Hissing Cockroach

- insect
- found in most tropical regions
- lives mostly on the forest floor

The Madagascan hissing cockroach has no wings, but it is a fast climber. It can grow up to 5–7.5 centimeters (2–3 inches) long. To warn its enemies, the cockroach makes a hissing sound by forcing air through holes in its abdomen.

This cockroach has an important role in the rain forest habitat. It eats decaying plant and animal matter. It breaks the matter down for reuse in nature.

▲ The Madagascan hissing cockroach has a glossy black and reddish-brown back.

Postman Butterfly

- insect
- found in South America
- lives in the canopy

The postman butterfly begins as a caterpillar, which hatches from an egg. The caterpillar looks like bird droppings, which can fool its predators. If an animal does approach, the caterpillar has a second line of defense. It lets off a highly unpleasant smell.

The caterpillar eats passionflower leaves, which make the adult butterfly poisonous to predators. The butterfly's bright colors tell birds and other predators of its danger. As an adult, the postman butterfly eats mostly flower nectar.

▲ The postman butterfly's bright markings are a warning to predators.

Resplendent Quetzal

- bird
- found in Mexico and Central America
- lives in the understory

The resplendent quetzal is named for the brilliant colors of the male. Most of his body is vivid green, while his breast is a rich crimson. The male has a long train of tail feathers. These feathers can grow as long as 61 centimeters (24 inches). He will flutter these feathers in front of a female quetzal to impress her. In cycles, the tail feathers fall out and then grow back again.

The ancient Maya and Aztec people of Central America and Mexico believed that the quetzal was a special bird that should be protected.

◄ The resplendent quetzal is one of the world's most beautiful birds.

Scarlet Macaw

- bird
- found in Central and South America
- lives in the canopy and emergent level

The scarlet macaw is a large type of parrot. It grows to about 90 centimeters (35 inches) long. It is named for its bright red feathers.

Scarlet macaws eat seeds, nuts, and fruits. They nest in holes high up in trees. They often travel in pairs or small flocks and can fly at speeds of up to 56 kilometers (35 miles) per hour.

Scarlet macaws have suffered from habitat loss and from their capture for the pet trade. They are now an endangered species.

▲ Scarlet macaws form pair bonds, which they keep for life.

Sloth

- mammal
- found in Central and South America
- lives in the understory

The sloth is one of the world's slowest moving creatures. Sloths are known for their unusual appearance. They have blunt snouts, very small ears and tails, and peg-like teeth.

Sloths are also known to sleep a lot. They can spend up to 18 hours a day sleeping. They spend most of their time up in the trees. They use their hook-like claws to hang onto branches. They tend to go unnoticed by predators as they hang there quietly.

◄ The sloth likes to hang upside down.

Tarantula

- arachnid
- found in South America
- lives on the forest floor and in the lower parts of the understory

A tarantula is a large hairy spider. The bird spider of South America, one of the world's largest spiders, is a tarantula. It has a body that is 7.6–10 centimeters (3–4 inches) long, and it can spread its legs about 18 centimeters (7 inches).

Tarantulas hunt at night. They crush their prey using their large fangs. Then they inject digestive juices into the body and suck up the liquid.

▲ Bird spiders are tarantulas that live in trees and eat small birds.

Tapir

- mammal
- found in South and Central America and Southeast Asia
- lives on the forest floor

Tapirs are medium-sized, pig-like animals with a smooth coat and a streamlined shape. Their shape lets them move easily through dense rain forest undergrowth.

Tapirs have an excellent sense of smell. Their nostrils are at the end of their trunk-like nose and help them locate food on the forest floor. This nose also helps tapirs hide from predators. They can hide underwater with only their trunk sticking out, and breathe through it like a snorkel.

▲ Tapirs use their long snouts and keen sense of smell to help them find food.

Apply the **Key Concepts**

Key Concept 1 Animals interact with their environment and with other animals in their habitats.

Activity Choose two animals that live in the rain forest. Find out how each of these animals uses their environment to live. Draw them in their habitats. Write captions that tell how they live in the rain forest.

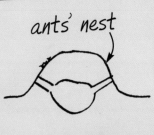

ants' nest

Key Concept 2 There are many different habitats on Earth. Animals live in habitats that meet their needs.

Activity Choose two animals that live in the rain forest. Find out how each of these animals uses plants to live. Then draw a Venn diagram to show what is the same and what is different.

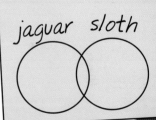

jaguar   sloth

Key Concept 3 Adaptations help animals survive in their habitats.

Activity Choose four animals that live in the rain forest. Use this book to find out about the adaptations that help each animal find food, shelter, and protection. Tell whether each adaptation is a physical or behavioral adaptation.

Rain Forest
Animals
1. tarantula
2.
3.
4.

Create Your Own Encyclopedia

Lots of animals live in the rain forest. You have read about some of them. Now it's time to find out about more of them. Get ready to do some research. Then get ready to make a book about rain forest animals. You can work with others to make a group book.

1. Study the Model

Look back at pages 19–26. Pick one animal you think is interesting. Now look closely at the entry for that animal. What facts are included? Do these tell what the animal eats? Where it sleeps? How it protects itself? These are the kinds of facts you might want to include in your entry.

Encyclopedia Entries

- Each entry is about one person, place, or thing.
- Use a title to say what the entry is about.
- Use pictures with labels to show what things look like.
- Include important facts.

2. Choose Your Topic

You can't write about what you do not know. So start by looking through books about rain forest animals. Look at the pictures. Read about animals that look interesting. For each animal, ask yourself:

- What is special about this animal?
- What facts are important?
- Does the picture show what the animal looks like?

List the animals that you think are interesting.

Then pick the one you'd like to learn more about.

3. Research Your Topic

Question

Ask yourself what you know. Ask yourself what you want to know. Make a list of questions. Use this list to guide your research. To find facts about your animal, look through books. Go on the Internet.

Take Notes

Keep track of what you find out. Take notes. Use a chart to help you sort your notes. Make copies of pictures you might want to use.

Topic: Siamang

1. Where does it live?

2. What does it eat?

3. How does it communicate?

4.

4. Write a Draft

Look over the facts you found. Now look back at one of the entries on pages 19–26. Use it as a model for writing about your animal. Be sure to use the important facts you collected. Also, include any interesting or weird facts about your animal.

5. Revise and Edit

Read your draft. What do you like? What would you like to change? Make these changes. Then read your draft again. This time, fix any mistakes. Look for words that are misspelled. Be sure each sentence starts with a capital letter.

Create Your Own Book

Now you can share your work. Get together with others to make a class book. Follow the steps below.

How to Make a Book

1. **Check that each entry has a title.**
   The title should name the animal.
2. **Include a photo or drawing for each entry.**
   Use a photo you found. Or you can draw a picture of your animal.
3. **Add captions to pictures.**
   Remember, captions and labels tell what pictures are about.
4. **Organize the entries alphabetically.**
   Look at the title of each entry. Put them in alphabetical order.
5. **Number the pages.**
   Add the page number for each page.
6. **Prepare a table of contents.**
   Look at the table of contents in this and other books. Now make one for your book.
7. **Make a cover.**
   Talk with your group about what you want on your cover. Choose pictures that tell what the book is about. Talk about a title. Then make your cover.
8. **Now bind the pages together.**
   You can staple the pages together. Or you can punch holes on the left side and tie the pages together with yarn.

Dolphin
- mammal
- lives in the sunlit zone

Dolphins do not breathe underwater.

2

Stinkbug
- insect
- found in most parts of the world
- lives on the forest floor

Stinkbugs suck food from leaves

Animal Encyclopedia

Glossary

adaptation – a body part or the way an animal acts to help it survive

behavioral adaptations – the things an animal does, such as get food or make shelter, to help it survive

camouflage – the way an animal changes how it looks to blend into its surroundings

climate – what the general weather conditions are like in a certain area

community – a group of plants and animals living together in a habitat

foliage – the leaves of plants

generation – animals that are born around the same time, often to one set of parents

habitat – the place where an animal or plant usually lives in nature

inherited – when an animal's trait is with it from birth because its parents have the same trait

mimicry – when an animal species has copied a trait of another species

organisms – forms of life

oxygen – a gas with no color or smell that animals and plants need to live

physical adaptations – the ways an animal's body changes to help it survive

predators – animals that hunt other animals for food

trait – a feature of an animal species that makes it different from other species

Index